PARROT

1

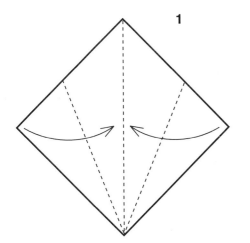

2

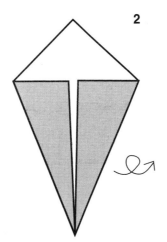

3

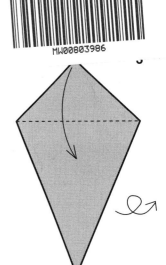

4

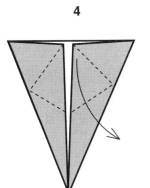

5

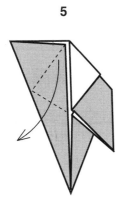

6

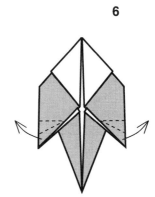

7

8

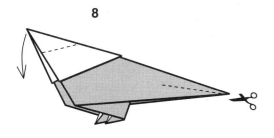

9

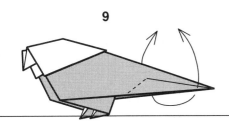

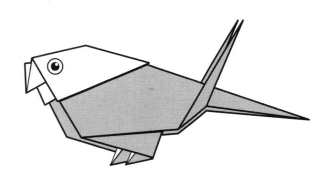

COLOR ME

See the back cover for color reference

HOUSE FINCH

FERRUGINOUS HAWK

RUBY-THROATED HUMMINGBIRD

ROSE-BREASTED GROSBEAK

COPY THIS DRAWING OF WORLD'S LARGEST AND FASTEST BIRD, THE OSTRICH, BY DRAWING IT ONE SQUARE AT A TIME

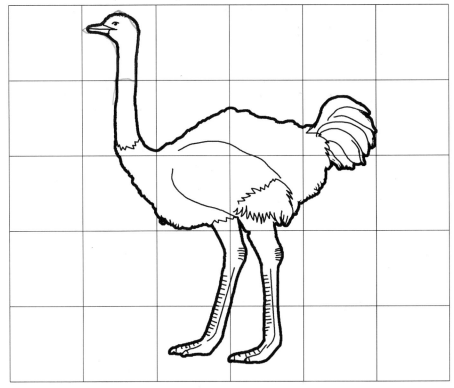

**HELP THE BARN OWL
FIND THE DEER MOUSE**

WORD SEARCH

COMMON BACKYARD BIRDS

```
H U M M I N G B I R D I R G R
K H N L B L U E B I R D N K R
K G I W E L W F R O K I I W E
H I T D O E A H O N L I O W G
O F R I B R D O N R W R R O I
U F A C E A C A A L R N L L O
S L M G R I R T K A T D R A K
E I E K R S N P C F U B N N
F C L O I S S S I I L T I P
I K P R O N E N N W U H I D G
N E R S M S G C K E A T C R M
C R U H U E H L J F I L H A N
H H P O L H L A E I B R L C N
O A H W L I Y A O T N I B O R
N E R W E S U O H D E I S H W
```

HUMMINGBIRD

CROW

FLICKER

ROBIN

PURPLE MARTIN

HOUSE WREN

CARDINAL

BARN SWALLOW

STARLING

CHICKADEE

BLUEBIRD

HOUSE FINCH

KINGLET

HOUSE SPARROW

GOLDFINCH

BLUE JAY

SOLUTION

```
M H S I E D H O U S E W R E N
O A H W L I Y A O T N I B O R
N E R S M S G C K E A T C R M
N H U H U E H L F I L H H O
M W S G C K E A T O U E
G L O I S S S I I L F K
N E K R S N P C F U B S E
K M G R I R T K A T D L R
O C E A C A A L R N L I F
I B R D O N R W R R O I O
G H O E A H O N L I O W T I
E L W F R O K I I W E K N
H L B L U E B I R D N K H
R I R D B I R G N I M M U H
```

NAME SCRAMBLE

UNSCRAMBLE THE NAMES OF THESE AFRICAN BIRDS

L O N R I H B L
1

L W O
2

G I N H R E K S I F
3

O W W A L L S
4

G E A E L
5

V A E N R
6

R R O A T P
7

V E R T U L U
8

O G E N P I
9

R E S T E K L
10

1. Hornbill   2. Owl   3. Kingfisher   4. Swallow   5. Eagle   6. Raven   7. Parrot   8. Vulture   9. Pigeon   10. Kestrel

NAME MATCH

DRAW A LINE BETWEEN THE BIRD AND ITS NAME

1

2

3

4

5

6

7

WOODPECKER

PRAIRIE FALCON

HOODED MERGANSER

LIMPKIN

WHITE PELICAN

WHITE IBIS

CROW

REDHEAD

BARN SWALLOW

WHIMBREL

CHUKAR

VIRGINIA RAIL

WREN

STELLER'S JAY

8

9

10

11

12

13

14

WORD SEARCH

GREAT LAKES BIRDS

REDPOLL

TUFTED TITMOUSE

PINE SISKIN

INDIGO BUNTING

DARK-EYED JUNCO

BANK SWALLOW

```
R W K R O E N E I B L E W I R E D
C E I R O G L B O A K T O G E A C
G A H L A I I D O L I I L B G I G
C N T S D L S I E T N H L I F E K
L O I B A T D L L I G W A E O I C
A L W T I R U E G M L B W O L C C
W O O B N R H R N O E O S P C K P
T D O P I U D T K R T B K E O N E
K B D B D R B A H E O O N G P I U
D R P L O E D O B O Y H A H R G O
O V E N B I R D G R O I B N N N D
I A C R P I N E S I S K I N A I W
R E K S R R R W O O D T H R U S H
T I E S U O R G W L N N T H T N N
T H R T R A T S D E R R I V O N R
R E S U O M T I T D E T F U T L M
I H W O O E R I V G N I L B R A W
```

BOBWHITE

WILD TURKEY

GROUSE

REDSTART

GRAY CATBIRD

WOOD THRUSH

HORNED LARK

KINGLET

INDIGO BUNTING

BALTIMORE ORIOLE

COWBIRD

OVENBIRD

SOLUTION

WOODPECKER

WARBLING VIREO

BROWN THRASHER

SHADOW KNOW-HOW

CAN YOU IDENTIFY THESE COMMON BIRDS?

SPOT THE DIFFERENCES

CAN YOU SPOT SIX DIFFERENCES BETWEEN THE RUBY-THROATED HUMMINGBIRDS?

WHO AM I?

1 	**2** 	**3** 	**4** 
5 	**6** 	**7** 	**8** 
9 	**10** 	**11** 	**12** 
13 	**14** 	**15** 	**16** 

BONUS QUESTION: Who is an endangered bird of prey?

1. Raven
2. Rock Dove
3. Grouse
4. Quail
5. Woodpecker
6. Crow
7. Jay
8. Hawk
9. Turkey
10. Condor
11. Sparrow
12. Swallow
13. Owl
14. Kingfisher
15. Hummingbird
16. Roadrunner

Bonus: #10

PICTURE SCRAMBLE

ARRANGE NUMBERS IN THE LETTERED BOXES
TO CREATE THE IMAGE ON THE LEFT

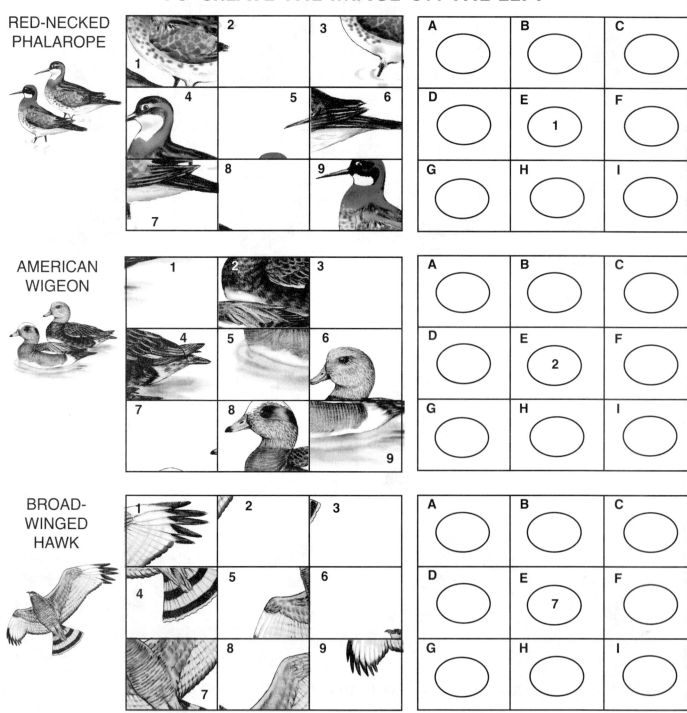

RED-NECKED PHALAROPE

AMERICAN WIGEON

BROAD-WINGED HAWK

WORD SEARCH

BIRDS OF PREY

BLACK VULTURE

BALD EAGLE

U	L	A	G	E	O	W	A	R	A	K	N	E	Y	A
K	W	E	S	R	R	A	F	U	D	C	L	N	A	L
L	O	E	B	T	P	S	S	W	A	L	O	K	W	K
E	G	O	B	B	L	U	O	R	S	C	A	O	L	C
L	N	A	A	E	L	W	A	A	L	E	L	W	E	O
G	I	A	R	B	S	C	O	A	A	A	R	W	R	I
A	W	G	L	P	A	N	F	N	E	K	A	Y	T	L
E	O	R	O	R	O	T	A	R	R	A	A	Y	S	C
N	R	A	A	K	R	R	O	I	R	A	E	Y	E	Y
E	R	Y	O	L	E	B	L	E	L	V	B	O	K	R
D	U	H	E	R	U	T	L	U	V	K	C	A	L	B
L	B	A	L	D	E	A	G	L	E	I	I	A	F	Y
O	D	W	L	K	W	O	R	N	D	W	G	T	A	C
G	A	K	C	Y	C	O	S	P	R	E	Y	E	E	E
N	E	L	W	O	Y	W	O	N	S	U	U	I	N	R

BOREAL OWL

BARN OWL

GOLDEN EAGLE

KESTREL

GRAY HAWK

BURROWING
OWL

SNOWY OWL

FALCON

SNAIL KITE

OSPREY

CARACARA

13

NAME MATCH

DRAW A LINE BETWEEN THE BIRD AND ITS NAME

1

2

3

4

5

6

7

PINE GROSBEAK

CHIMNEY SWIFT

YELLOWTHROAT

NORTHERN FLICKER

ELF OWL

PAINTED BUNTING

OSPREY

TREE SPARROW

SAGE GROUSE

CANYON WREN

AMERICAN KESTREL

CLIFF SWALLOW

MOURNING DOVE

RUBY-THROATED HUMMINGBIRD

8

9

10

11

12

13

14

MAZES

BLACK SKIMMERS FEED BY FLYING OVER THE WATER WITH THEIR LOWER BEAK 'SKIMMING' THE SURFACE UNTIL THEY CONTACT A FISH.

THE CHICKADEE IS A SMALL BACKYARD BIRD THAT SINGS ITS NAME – *CHICK-A-DEE-DEE-DEE*. YOU CAN MAKE AT LEAST 15 WORDS FROM THE LETTERS IN ITS NAME.

CHICKADEE

_____   _____

_____   _____

_____   _____

_____   _____

_____   _____

_____   _____

Answer: had, hide, cake, ace, ice, die, dike, hike, deck, head, heed, cheek, idea, chick, check.

AUSTRALIAN BIRDS
See the back cover for color reference.

COMB-CRESTED JACANA

DOLLARBIRD

CHESTNUT-BREASTED MANNIKIN

SACRED KINGFISHER

MAZES

HELP THIS TINY ELF OWL FIND A SAGUARO CACTUS TO NEST IN

ODDBALL OUT

IN EACH ROW, CIRCLE THE BIRD WHICH IS DIFFERENT FROM THE OTHERS

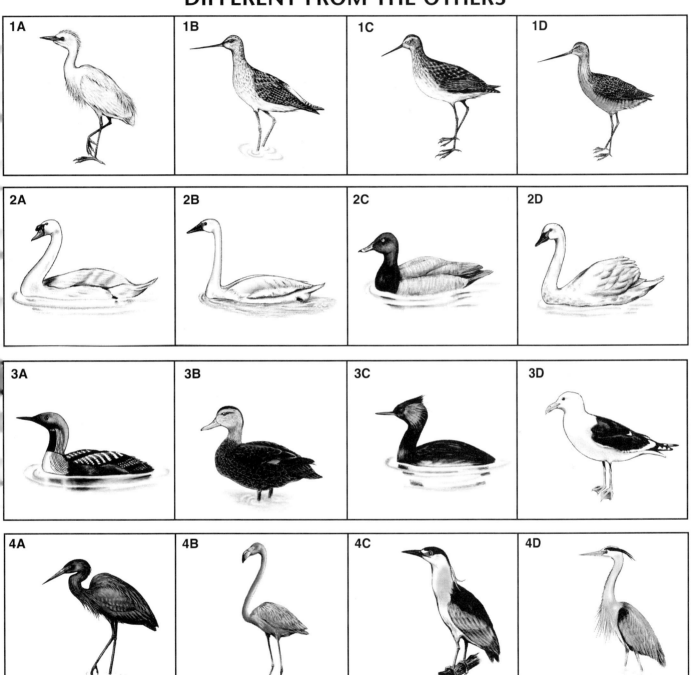

BONUS QUESTION: Which bird's body is the color of its food?

1B, 1C & 1D are sandpipers; 1A is an egret
3A, 3B & 3C are waterfowl; 3D is a gull
Bonus: 4B. The flamingo eats shrimp.

2A, 2B & 2D are swans; 2C is a duck
4A, 4C & 4D are herons; 4B is a flamingo

CAN YOU IDENTIFY THESE BIRDS BY THEIR BILLS?

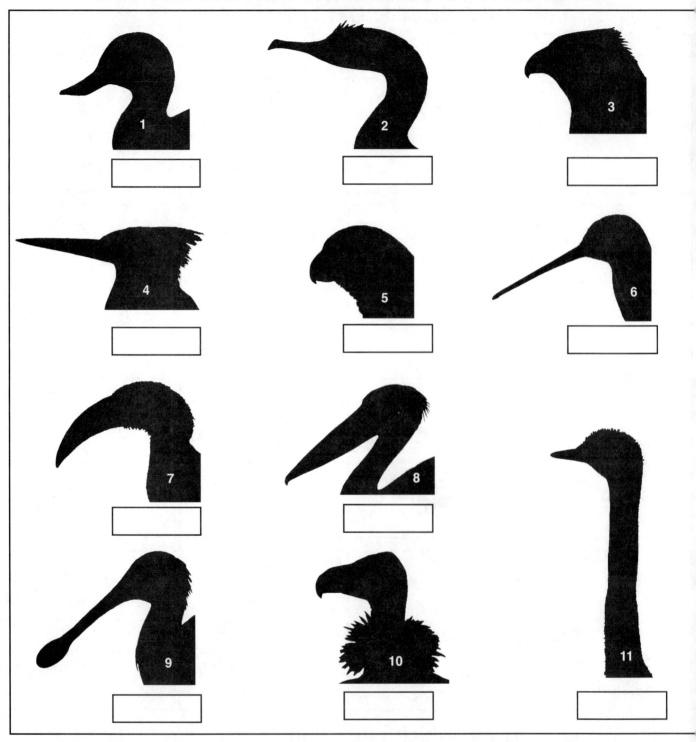

1. Duck
2. Cormorant
3. Eagle
4. Kingfisher
5. Parrot
6. Snipe
7. Hornbill
8. Pelican
9. Spoonbill
10. Vulture
11. Ostrich

WORD SEARCH

AFRICAN BIRDS

HERON

```
N U B E N G N G O O S E U N E
B R A K N O B Y R A N A C O V
U O B P G O R R W G R R E D E
T N U N R C T N A R O M R O C
N A O T U I E S B T F O L G O
I R K R R N E G N T R A R F C
D N C T I U R G U R B O L H N
U O I T E R R R R G U Y G I N
U A H R E B A U N E C T U O D
H N C E N C R L N A B G Q H N
E T B V O B N A T E N E U N G
R D A A R A E C B E E E T G
O U D E B R H T P N R S L N A
N U N W D E O D G E S D E R H
O I K S R S U N B I R D A N R
```

DABCHICK

PENGUIN

TURNSTONE

QUELEA

HERON

GREBE

GOOSE

CANARY

SUNBIRD

WEAVER

FLYCATCHER

CORMORANT

TROGON

BARBET

DRONGO

TURACO

SOLUTION

NAME MATCH

DRAW A LINE BETWEEN THE BIRD AND ITS NAME

1

2

3

4

5

6

7

COMMON GOLDENEYE

AMERICAN WIGEON

WHITE-WINGED SCOTER

NORTHERN PINTAIL

BLUE-WINGED TEAL

GREEN-WINGED TEAL

BUFFLEHEAD

RING-NECKED DUCK

NORTHERN SHOVELER

CANVASBACK

RUDDY DUCK

LESSER SCAUP

MALLARD

HARLEQUIN DUCK

 **8**

 **9**

 **10**

 **11**

 **12**

 **13**

 **14**

1. American wigeon
2. Ring-necked duck
3. Northern pintail
4. Canvasback
5. Mallard
6. Bufflehead
7. Blue-winged teal
8. Northern shoveler
9. Common goldeneye
10. Ruddy duck
11. White-winged scoter
12. Green-winged teal
13. Harlequin duck
14. Lesser scaup

MAZES

HELP THE GREAT EGRET FIND A CLAM FOR SUPPER

NAME SCRAMBLE

UNSCRAMBLE THE NAMES OF THESE COMMON BIRDS

N O R I B

1

C F N I H

2

A A R N T G E

3

E B D L R U I B

4

G S O U E R

5

W L S W O L A

6

N G O P E I

7

O N R C D O

8

A W R B E R L

9

A R S T G N I L

10

PICTURE SCRAMBLE

ARRANGE NUMBERS IN THE LETTERED BOXES
TO CREATE THE IMAGE ON THE LEFT

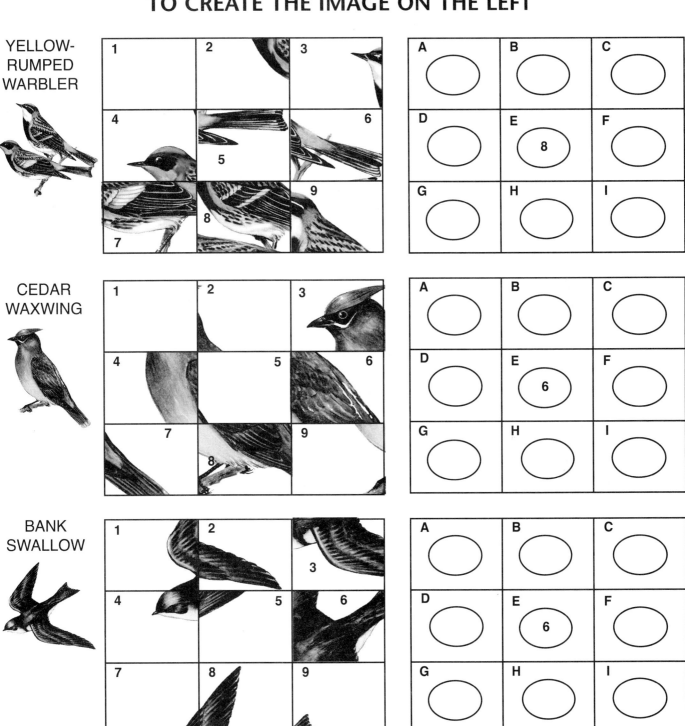

YELLOW-RUMPED WARBLER

CEDAR WAXWING

BANK SWALLOW

Bank swallow - A7, B8, C9, D1, E6, F5, G4, H3, I2
Cedar waxwing - A3, B2, C1, D4, E6, F5, G9, H8, I7
Yellow-rumped warbler - A3, B9, C1, D4, E8, F6, G2, H7, I5

ODDBALL OUT

IN EACH ROW, CIRCLE THE BIRD WHICH IS DIFFERENT FROM THE OTHERS

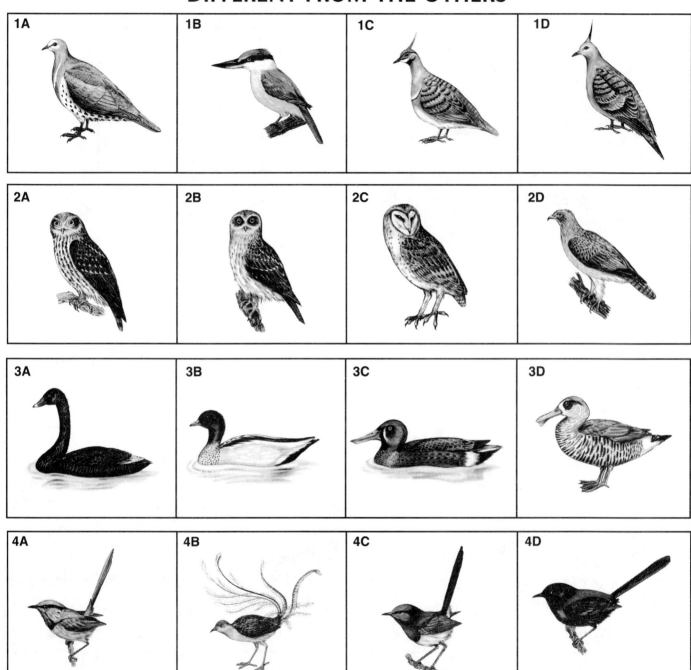

1A **1B** **1C** **1D**

2A **2B** **2C** **2D**

3A **3B** **3C** **3D**

4A **4B** **4C** **4D**

3A, 1C & 1D are pigeons; 1B is a kingfisher

2A, 2B & 2C are owls; 2D is an eagle

3B, 3C & 3D are ducks; 3A is a swan

4A, 4C & 4D are wrens; 4B is a lyrebird

WORD SEARCH

AUSTRALIAN NEARSHORE BIRDS

```
Y R A G L O R B N D O D C N T
P E N G U I N G A K Y S R E B
P L E G T C T E W J S O R L A
C E T E E A H A S G T G R W F
O B L T S D E P K N E L C R J
R L A I R O C A C O R O I H A
O K L A C E O N A I C G R D C
L R H I N A S G L G A I B S A
R O R I B E N K B T T E A V N
P T O T I N L I E N C I O A A
H S O H L B O B A O H C I C S
R G N N D S I O T L E H H D O
S E A B C R E S P T R L J L G
N O A G D I S B A S T E R N L
A E L O C N I T A R P N R H C
```

BLACK SWAN

FRIGATEBIRD

GOOSE

JACANA

PENGUIN

STORK

AVOCET

PRATINCOLE

BROLGA

PELICAN

OYSTERCATCHER

SPOONBILL

HARDHEAD

IBIS

EGRET

TERN

SOLUTION

```
A E L O C N I T A R P N R H C
N O A G D I S B A S T E R N L
S E A B C R E S P T R L J L G
R G N N D S I O T L E H H D O
H S O H L B O B A O H C I C S
P T O T I N L I E N C I O A A
R O R I B E N K B T T E A V N
L R H I N A S G L G A I B S A
O K L A C E O N A I C G R D C
R L A I R O C A C O R O I H A
O B L T S D E P K N E L C R J
C E T E E A H A S G T G R W F
P L E G T C T E W J S O R L A
P E N G U I N G A K Y S R E B
Y R A G L O R B N D O D C N T
```

1

2

3

4

5

6

7

8

9

10

11

12

13

14

15

16

BONUS QUESTION: Which bird drills holes in trees?

1. Grebe	5. Pelican	9. Spoonbill	13. Pigeon
2. Eider duck	6. Bittern	10. Vulture	14. Woodpecker
3. Wood duck	7. Woodcock	11. Kestrel	15. Warbler
4. Snow goose	8. Oystercatcher	12. Pheasant	16. Nuthatch

Bonus: # 14

FOLD-INS

FOLD THE PANELS FROM RIGHT TO LEFT
TO REVEAL A FAMOUS BIRD

C→   Fold   ←C   B→   Fold   ←B   A→   Fold   ←A

B A   D   G F   L D   I J

ZY   E A   D X   Y   G L   MS   EA   E

PICTURE SCRAMBLE

ARRANGE NUMBERS IN THE LETTERED BOXES
TO CREATE THE IMAGE ON THE LEFT

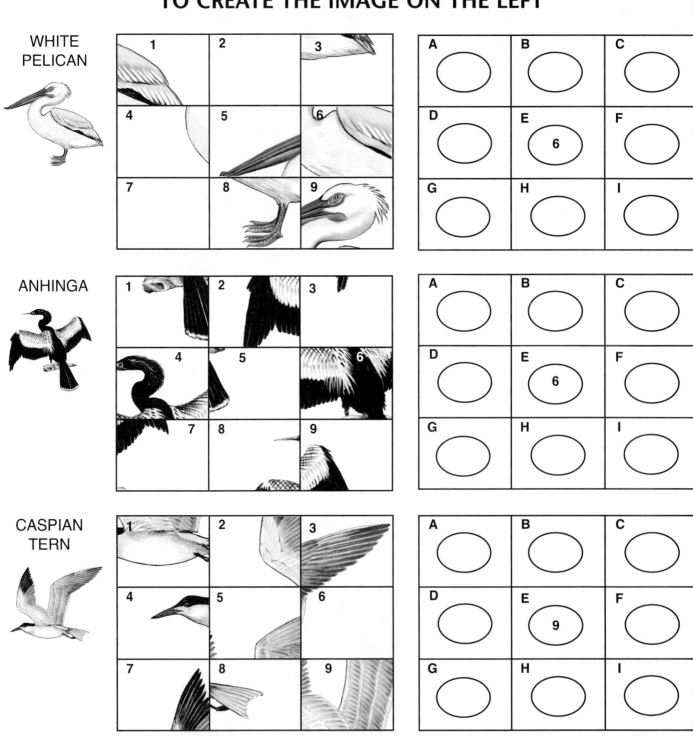

WHITE PELICAN

ANHINGA

CASPIAN TERN

SPOT THE DIFFERENCES

CAN YOU SPOT SIX DIFFERENCES BETWEEN THE GREAT BLUE HERONS?

1. Bill color 2. Eye color 3. Head plumes 4. Breast feathers 5. Shoulder marking 6. Leg position

NAME SCRAMBLE

UNSCRAMBLE THE NAMES OF THESE COMMON BIRDS

AALLDRM

1

KIDLLERE

2

BAKKUDCCL

3

ENORH

4

NWAS

5

HOTEWE

6

LGUL

7

VODE

8

SHIKEIFGNB

9

NHAAIGN

10

1. Mallard 2. Killdeer 3. Black duck 4. Heron 5. Swan 6. Towhee 7. Gull 8. Dove 9. Kingfisher 10. Anhinga

SWAN

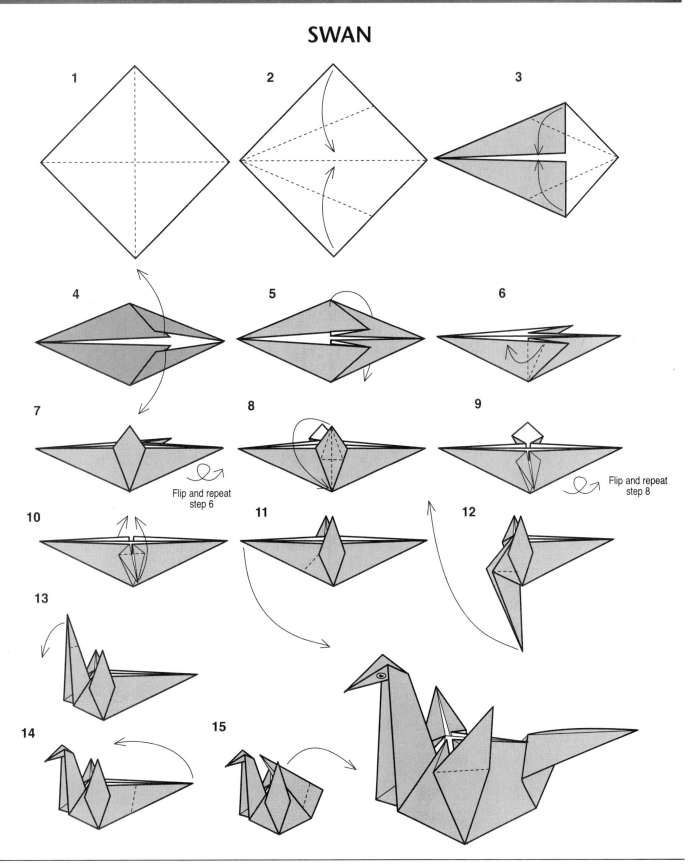

1

2

3

4

5

6

7

Flip and repeat
step 6

8

9

Flip and repeat
step 8

10

11

12

13

14

15

COLOR ME

AFRICAN BIRDS
See the back cover for color reference.

LILAC-BREASTED ROLLER

NARINA TROGON

GREAT BLUE TURACO

SPOT-BACKED WEAVER

NAME MATCH

DRAW A LINE BETWEEN THE AUSTRALIAN BIRD AND ITS NAME

MAGPIE GOOSE

LYREBIRD

PINK-EARED DUCK

KINGFISHER

BROLGA

BLACK SWAN

BUDGERIGAR

RAVEN

BRUSH-TURKEY

CASSOWARY

SULPHUR-CRESTED COCKATOO

LITTLE EAGLE

COCKATIEL

FAIRY-WREN

1. Magpie goose 2. Pink-eared duck 3. Black swan 4. Brolga 5. Budgerigar 6. Cockatiel 7. Sulphur-crested cockatoo 8. Sacred kingfisher 9. Lyrebird 10. Raven 11. Cassowary 12. Brush-turkey 13. Fairy-wren 14. Little eagle

HELP THE TOWHEE FIND A TREAT TO EAT

DRAW THIS VULTURE ONE SQUARE AT A TIME

NAME SCRAMBLE

UNSCRAMBLE THE NAMES OF THESE COMMON AFRICAN BIRDS

N R E T

1

U L Q A I

2

I L O R H L N B

3

O F M N G A L I

4

O E G O S

5

E N P U G N I

6

E H O P O O

7

E E E E R T B A

8

R H S C T O I

9

A E N P C I L

10

1. Tern 2. Quail 3. Hornbill 4. Flamingo 5. Goose 6. Penguin 7. Hoopoe 8. Bee-Eater 9. Ostrich 10. Pelican

NAME MATCH

DRAW A LINE BETWEEN THE BIRD AND ITS NAME

1

2

3

4

5

6

7

8

9

10

11

12

13

14

AVOCET

GREBE

SPOONBILL

COOT

DUCK

STORK

EGRET

FRIGATEBIRD

HERON

GULL

IBIS

JACANA

BUSTARD

PENGUIN

ODDBALL OUT

IN EACH ROW, CIRCLE THE BIRD WHICH IS DIFFERENT FROM THE OTHERS

1A 1B 1C 1D

2A 2B 2C 2D

3A 3B 3C 3D

4A 4B 4C 4D

1A, 1C & 1D are loons; 1B is a grebe
2A, 2B & 2C are ducks; 2D is a coot

3A, 3C & 3D are puffins; 3B is a razorbill
4A, 4B & 4D are gulls; 4C is a tern

SHADOW KNOW-HOW

CAN YOU IDENTIFY THESE COMMON AFRICAN BIRDS?

1. Swallow
2. Eagle
3. Ostrich
4. Pin-tailed whydah
5. Vulture
6. Hornbill
7. Secretarybird
8. Kingfisher
9. Flamingo
10. Spoonbill
11. Heron

SPOT THE DIFFERENCES

CAN YOU SPOT SIX DIFFERENCES BETWEEN THE GRAY-CROWNED CRANES?

1. Crown shape   2. Eye shape   3. Cheek pattern   4. Bill shape   5. Right leg position   6. Tail color

WHO AM I?

BONUS QUESTION: Which Australian bird is the world's second largest bird?

1. Sandpiper
2. Kingfisher
3. Eagle
4. Tern
5. Emu
6. Cockatoo
7. Cormorant
8. Wren
9. Budgerigar
10. Rock dove
11. Swan
12. Owl
13. Turkey
14. Duck
15. Cockatiel
16. Pelican

Bonus: #5

THE TURNSTONE USES ITS BEAK TO TURN OVER STONES AND OTHER OBJECTS WHEN SEARCHING FOR FOOD. CAN YOU HELP THE TURNSTONE FIND SOME LUNCH?

BE AN ARTIST

COPY THIS HUMMINGBIRD BY DRAWING IT
ONE SQUARE AT A TIME

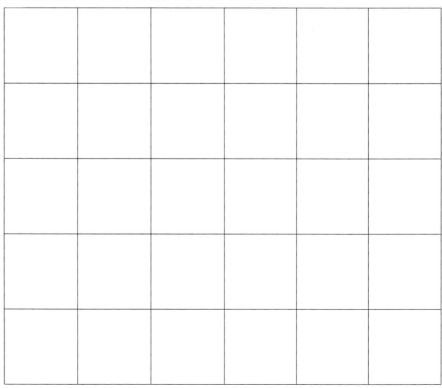

WORD SEARCH

ROCKY MOUNTAIN BIRDS

```
E R S O N G S P A R R O W B T I
L L I B S S O R C D E R I R L R
K E D U G O G E C I P R J C C R
A T R L N N L A O H E R L K R Y
E A O L R I I H B P U I W T U T
B O P O K M H W E N F K P O G O
S R N C H C E E X F E I A N R W
O H I K C C R A S A N V I R D H
R T G S N C T W D Y W T A I O E
G W H O E R A A O O N R P R L E
O O T R K L D N H U W P A L O W
L L H I L N J L B T E L A D H A
A L A O T A O W E R U B A O E S
E E W L Y I O E E D O N E R N C
R Y K E E N R G R A C K L E K T
O A D S S D R I B G N I K A E I
```

GROSBEAK

SONG SPARROW

RED CROSSBILL

BULLOCK'S ORIOLE

SNOW BUNTING

TOWHEE

RAVEN

CHUKAR

MEADOWLARK

DIPPER

NIGHTHAWK

YELLOWTHROAT

CLIFF SWALLOW

NUTHATCH

CREEPER

KINGBIRD

PINYON JAY

GRACKLE

CEDAR WAXWING

SOLUTION

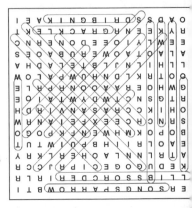

CONNECT-THE-DOTS

LINK THE NUMBERS TO HELP THE KINGFISHER FIND ITS DINNER

WORD SEARCH

COMMON NEARSHORE BIRDS

ANHINGA

YELLOWLEGS

CLAPPER RAIL

```
E O R L N O E G I W W R W L R
R S L S I B B A A O W O O E R
I S E I I A T E L D O Y H S E
C A S A A O T L P D W S W O L
B C G H O R A N D I I A O O B
L A E C P W R U I F N S L G R
A N L C S S C E G P P S C L A
C V W G N K I N P R C O W E W
K A O N A C I L E P E T I H W
D S L K R K P Y D S A B A R L
U B L A L O O N A N W L G W O
C A E A D R A L L A M A C R I
K C Y I O A N H I N G A N G O
S K C R G R E A T E G R E T O
E T E R P A D A E H D E R S A
```

GOOSE

SWAN

COOT

CANVASBACK

SNIPE

BLACK DUCK

GADWALL

PINTAIL

REDHEAD

WIGEON

LOON

MALLARD

WHITE PELICAN

WOOD DUCK

WARBLER

SOLUTION

GREAT EGRET

KINGFISHER

OSPREY

SWALLOW

COMMON AUSTRALIAN PARROTS
See the back cover for color reference.

BUDGERIGAR

CRIMSON ROSELLA

RAINBOW LORIKEET

COCKATIEL

1

2

3

4

5

6

7

8

9

10

11

12

13

14

15

16

1. Loon
2. Egret
3. Puffin
4. Pelican

5. Anhinga
6. Sandpiper
7. Swan
8. Gull

9. Wood duck
10. Tern
11. Flamingo
12. Cormorant

13. Crane
14. Goose
15. Grebe
16. Heron

ODDBALL OUT

IN EACH ROW, CIRCLE THE BIRD THAT IS DIFFERENT FROM THE OTHERS

1A 1B 1C 1D

2A 2B 2C 2D

3A 3B 3C 3D

4A 4B 4C 4D

1A, 1C & 1D are waterfowl; 1B is a shorebird
2A, 2B & 2C are shorebirds; 2D is a forest bird

3A, 3C & 3D are egrets; 3B is a heron
4A, 4B & 4D are cormorants; 4C is an anhinga

SHADOW KNOW-HOW

CAN YOU IDENTIFY THESE AUSTRALIAN BIRDS?

CONNECT-THE-DOTS

BIRDS OF PREY HAVE CURVED TALONS FOR GRASPING PREY, HOOKED BEAKS FOR TEARING FLESH, AND GOOD EYESIGHT TO HELP THEM HUNT.

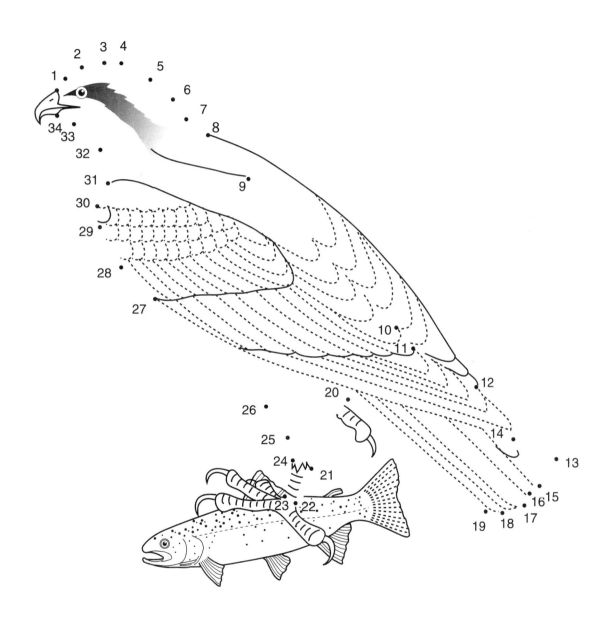

BONUS QUESTION: What is it?

Bonus: Osprey

FOLD-INS

**FOLD-IN THE PANELS FROM RIGHT TO LEFT TO REVEAL A
COMMON ROADSIDE BIRD OF PREY**

C→	Fold	←C	B→	Fold	←B	A→	Fold	←A

A	BL	TA	ME	DGF	HO	ERI	J KO	IC	CAN
	AM	THE	KE	ZY	W	ST	E	XY	REL

BE AN ARTIST

COPY THIS SWALLOW BY DRAWING IT ONE SQUARE AT A TIME

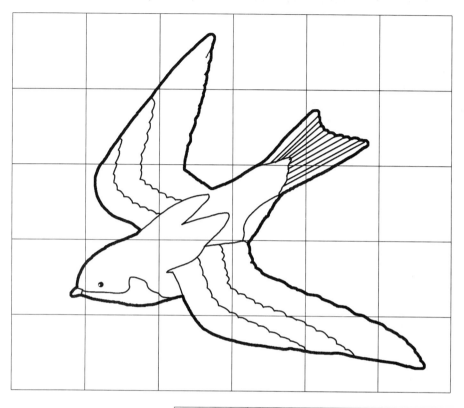

NAME SCRAMBLE

UNSCRAMBLE THE NAMES OF THESE BIRDS

KOSRT

1

KCDU

2

NNAERDSGIL

3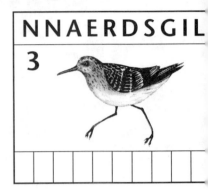

OTOC

4

REHNO

5

SOEGO

6

VORPLE

7

MMIKERS

8

TOEAVC

9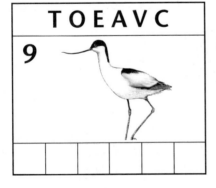

EERBG

10

1. Stork 2. Duck 3. Sanderling 4. Coot 5. Heron 6. Goose 7. Plover 8. Skimmer 9. Avocet 10. Grebe

PICTURE SCRAMBLE

ARRANGE NUMBERS IN THE LETTERED BOXES
TO CREATE THE IMAGE ON THE LEFT

ELF OWL

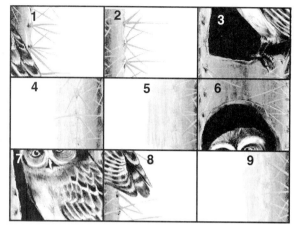

A	B	C
D	E	F
	7	
G	H	I

PEREGRINE FALCON

A	B	C
D	E	F
	9	
G	H	I

CALIFORNIA CONDOR

A	B	C
D	E	F
	1	
G	H	I

WORD SEARCH

AFRICAN NEARSHORE BIRDS

PELICAN

```
L N D L D N M A O A V R O M R
E R E T R A D V M E B I N S L
N D N P E L I C A N C O M T T
C E T E O C O O T C R R I C S
B B T E N A R C D E N W O R C
O O O L G E L A H S R A B S E
R R K L L I L P S R A I S L E
A E P A R I I E K K L M O O I
P R V V G C B S A I I G A J C
O E G O U E N E I N M A L L
L T O C L P O E O I I C M A L
C E D E L P H I M O A B L E A
R R S T S R S A R N P N I R R
R G J E C C L O A V C S I S E
E E C J N F P M L E N T P O T
```

GULL

DARTER

IBIS

SHOEBILL

EGRET

CROWNED CRANE

HERON

SKIMMER

FLAMINGO

COOT

SOLUTION

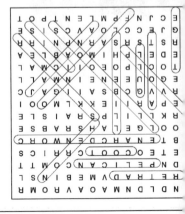

AVOCET

PLOVER

JACANA

SANDPIPER

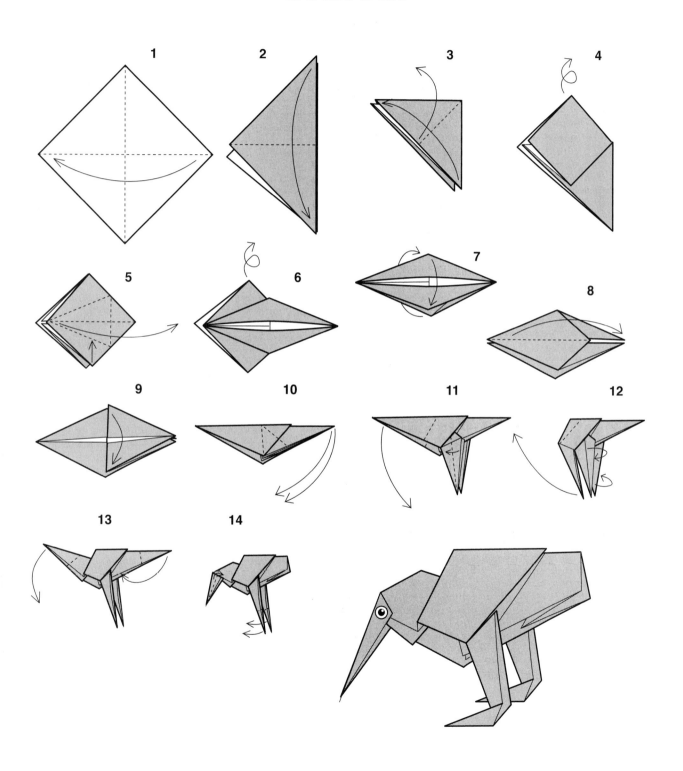

WHO AM I?

1. Goldeneye
2. Merganser
3. Northern pintail
4. Blue-winged teal
5. American wigeon
6. Mallard
7. Gadwall
8. Ring-necked duck
9. Wood duck
10. Ruddy duck
11. American black duck
12. Bufflehead
13. American coot
14. Pied-billed grebe
15. Canada goose
16. Tundra swan

NAME SCRAMBLE

UNSCRAMBLE THE NAMES OF THESE BIRDS OF PREY

LEURUVT
1

NDCOOR
2

GALEE
3

TIKE
4

CANOLF
5

KWAH
6

WOL
7

RSKEETL
8

ROEPSY
9
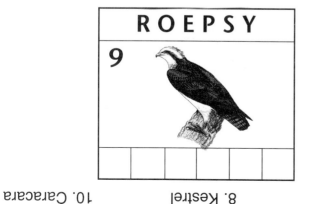

CAAACRRA
10

1. Vulture 2. Condor 3. Eagle 4. Kite 5. Falcon 6. Hawk 7. Owl 8. Kestrel 9. Osprey 10. Caracara

SPOT THE DIFFERENCES

CAN YOU SPOT FIVE DIFFERENCES BETWEEN THE ROCK DOVES?

Eye ring   2. Hood length   3. Wing bar missing   4. Foot color   5. Band at the tail tip

HELP THIS GULL FIND ITS FRIENDS

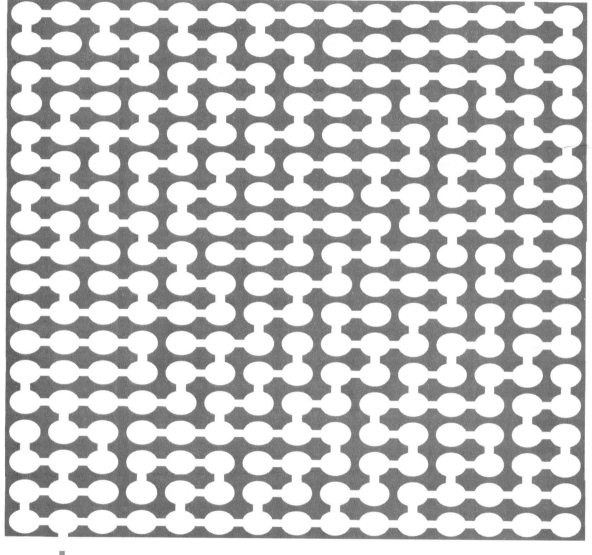

ODDBALL OUT

IN EACH ROW, CIRCLE THE BIRD WHICH IS DIFFERENT FROM THE OTHERS

1A 1B 1C 1D
2A 2B 2C 2D
3A 3B 3C 3D
4A 4B 4C 4D

1C & 1D are sparrows; 1B is a robin
2B & 2C are chickadees; 2D is a warbler

3A, 3C & 3D are woodpeckers; 3B is a creeper
4A, 4B & 4D are vultures; 4C is an eagle